PISTE OFF

A Play

by

Paul Beard

C   Paul Beard 1992

Published by:
New Playwrights' Network
35, Sandringham Road
Macclesfield
Cheshire
SK10 1QB

ISBN 0 86319 308 0

LINCOLNSHIRE
COUNTY COUNCIL

822

CHARACTERS

Robert

Brian

Clare

Kate

Piste Off is a comedy of character and situation for two men and two women.

The setting is a studio apartment in the French Alps during the skiing season where the snow has failed to arrive.

The overall appearance of the apartment should be one of a confined space, suitcases, clothing and ski equipment taking up much of the floor space.

Centre rear are bunk beds. Downstage right, a sofa divan. Downstage left is a room divider which conceals the kitchen area from the audience.

Entrance to the apartment is upstage right. Exit to the bathroom is upstage left.

PISTE OFF

Thursday. 6 a.m. ROBERT is asleep in the top bunk. CLARE is asleep in the bottom bunk. BRIAN and KATE are asleep on the sofa divan.

The room is in darkness, apart from a stream of light shining through from the kitchen area. An alarm bell sounds.

BRIAN: For Christ's sake turn that alarm clock off. There are people trying to sleep here.
KATE: I can't find it Brian. Where did you put it?
BRIAN: It was on the coffee table. Turn it off before you wake up the whole block. *(KATE gets out of bed and crawls to the coffee table, feeling her way in the dark as she does so)*
KATE: It's not there. I can't find it.
BRIAN: Switch the light on stupid. How do you expect to find it fumbling around in the dark? *(KATE moves upstage left to the entrance area)*
KATE: All right, don't shout. You'll wake the others up.
BRIAN: Well hurry up then, that bell's driving me nuts.
KATE: I can't find the light switch.
BRIAN: Oh, for crying out loud. It's by the door on the wall. It's been there all week. It hasn't suddenly decided to move position.
KATE: Shouting is not helping the situation Brian.
BRIAN: Put the table lamp on and you'll be able to see what you're doing.

KATE: I'm over here now. You're nearest, can't you?
BRIAN: Oh, for the love God, if you want a job doing, you might as well do it yourself. *(BRIAN gets out of bed and crawls to the coffee table and switches on the lamp. As he does, KATE switches on the main light)*
KATE: It's all right. I found it.
BRIAN: Brilliant.
ROBERT: Is it time to get up?
BRIAN: No, we thought we'd have a game of charades.
KATE: We can't find the clock
ROBERT: Oh, I've got it up here.
BRIAN: Well switch it off.
ROBERT: Oh, yes, sorry.
KATE: I nearly broke my neck looking for that. Why didn't you switch it off when it rang?
ROBERT: I didn't hear it. Sorry, it's these ear plugs.
BRIAN: Ear plugs. What's the point of having the alarm clock up there if you can't hear it. Why didn't you leave it on the coffee table so we could find it?
ROBERT: I thought I would hear it better up here. I didn't want to disturb you two. I set it early so I could see the sunrise.
KATE: Sunrise?
BRIAN: What's the time, for Christ's sake?
ROBERT: Well, it should be six o'clock.
KATE: Six o'clock!
BRIAN: It's the middle of the night. I'm, going back to bed.
CLARE: What's all the noise? What time is it?
BRIAN: Bedtime! *(BRIAN gets back into bed. CLARE gets out of bed)*
CLARE: Bonjour. Good morning one and all.
KATE: Sorry if we disturbed you Clare.
BRIAN: It's not morning, it's the middle of the night and if you lot wouldn't mind making a little less noise, I might be able to get some sleep.
ROBERT: Sorry.
CLARE: Was it something I said?
KATE: It's not your fault Clare. I think Brian's got one

of his heads this morning.
CLARE: I'm not surprised. He was drinking for England last night at the fondue evening.
ROBERT: It was a good night though, wasn't it?
KATE: Except for Brian.
ROBERT: He wasn't that bad.
CLARE: Yes he was, standing on the table leading the community singing. It's a wonder we didn't get asked to leave.
ROBERT: The New Zealanders thought he was funny.
KATE: Did they?
CLARE: No. They were laughing with embarrassment. They thought he was stupid.
BRIAN: Look, would you mind not talking about me as if I wasn't here. For your information I was not drunk last night, and I do not have a hangover. I do not get hangovers.
KATE: You always get a hangover when you're drunk.
BRIAN: I was not drunk.
KATE: You're always sick as well.
BRIAN: I'm never sick.
ROBERT: You were sick at our New Year's Eve party.
BRIAN: That was only once. Anyway, New Year is different. Everyone's sick on New Year's Eve, It's traditional.
CLARE: I'm not.
BRIAN: You don't get sick on mineral water.
ROBERT: I don't know. There was that trouble with Perrier..
CLARE: Shut up Robert.
ROBERT: Sorry I spoke.
KATE: I had to have the bathroom mat cleaned about twenty times last year.
BRIAN: Not because of me.
KATE: I told the lady in the cleaners that it was our dog.
ROBERT: You haven't got a dog.
KATE: It was the only thing I could think of at the time. I didn't want people to think that I am married to a man who is constantly vomiting over

PISTE OFF

          the bathroom mat.
BRIAN: Well, thank you very much. I'm a dog now am I?
CLARE: Cheer up Rover. Is it our turn to shower first this morning?
KATE: Yes. *(CLARE collects her clothes from a suitcase and exits to the bathroom)*
BRIAN: A bloody dog!
KATE: All right Brian, don't make a fuss. *(ROBERT gets out of bed and collects his clothes from a suitcase)*
ROBERT: Come on you two. This is supposed to be a holiday. No arguments. Remember?
BRIAN: We're not arguing Robert. Who's arguing? If we were arguing, Kate would be throwing things at me by now. No, this is just a mild disagreement. *(CLARE enters, wrapped in a towel)*
CLARE: Robert, are you ready for the shower?
ROBERT: Coming. Is it your turn to make the tea this morning Kate? *(KATE looks at a large rota which is pinned to the room divider. CLARE exits)*
KATE: Let's have a look. Thursday...tea...Kate...... yes, it's my turn.
ROBERT: Fine. Back in a tick. *(ROBERT exits to bathroom. BRIAN gets out of bed)*
BRIAN: If he mentions that rota one more time I'll flush it down the toilet. If you can call that thing a toilet.
KATE: What's wrong with the toilet?
BRIAN: A hole in the floor is not a toilet. A toilet should have a bowl, and a seat to sit on. That is a hole in the floor in my book.
KATE: I think their quite comfortable, actually. *(KATE takes clothes from suitcase and dresses)*
BRIAN: Comfortable! What's comfortable about having to squat like a three year old at the kerb, looking between your legs at yesterdays dinner, just to make sure it disappears down a hole in the floor?
KATE: Don't be disgusting.
BRIAN: Well, it's true. They're dangerous if you ask me. What would happen if you couldn't get your clothes

off in time.
KATE: You don't have to take your clothes off.
BRIAN: You might not. It's all right if you're wearing a skirt, but you try it with trousers. That's a different story, I can tell you. You never know what's going to end up in your back pocket.
KATE: You can really be disgusting, do you know that?
BRIAN: Stupid idea if you ask me. It's just another way to con us out of our money. They know that no self-respecting Englishman's going to be caught naked, squatting over a hole in the floor. So what do they do? They charge four francs to use a proper toilet down at the resort. They're not daft these French. Forty P for a crap! It's daylight robbery.
KATE: Then use the one here. I didn't save up all last year, just so you could flush it all down the loo.
BRIAN: Oh, very witty. Been thinking that one up all week have we?
KATE: Oh, for heaven's sake Brian. Cheer up. We're on holiday. We should be having fun.
BRIAN: Some fun this is. Four days we've been here and not a snowflake in sight. If this was a summer holiday, we would probably need a team of huskies to pull us around.
KATE: There's plenty of snow at other resorts.
BRIAN: A fat lot of good that is to us.
KATE: We could catch the curtsey bus like everybody else. At least we could do some skiing.
BRIAN: For the last time, I am not spending two hours on an overcrowded bus full of sweaty foreigners, just so I can put my skis on for five minutes then turn round and come back again. Besides, they only lay that on so they don't have to pay out under the guaranteed snow insurance. Well, I'm not falling for that one. I'd rather have the money.
KATE: What money?
BRIAN: It said in the brochure, that this resort has one of the best snow fall records in the region, didn't it?
KATE: Yes.

BRIAN: Well, because of that record they guarantee snow and, if there's not enough, you get a fifty pound refund. *(KATE picks up a brochure from the coffee table and throws it at BRIAN)*
KATE: If you read the small print Brian, it doesn't say anything about a lack of snow. It states a lack of lifts and there are plenty of lifts working.
BRIAN: Show me.
KATE: There.
BRIAN: Where?
KATE: See that little asterix there?
BRIAN: Yes.
KATE: And see that little asterix at the bottom of the next page, next to all that little writing?
BRIAN: That's criminal that is. I've a good mind to write to Judith Chalmers about this. Typical. I told you we should have gone to Scotland. At least they don't con you out of your money, and they speak the same language. Well, nearly. *(ROBERT and CLARE enter dressed in casual ski clothing)*
CLARE: Are you two still at it? Has the kettle boiled yet? I'm gasping.
ROBERT: Better hurry up you two. The water's getting cold.
BRIAN: How is it that when it's our turn to shower first, there's always hot water left for you, but when you two go first, it's cold for us.
CLARE: Probably because you shower together. We don't.
KATE: Don't you?
ROBERT: No, we do not.
BRIAN: Well you should. Perhaps then, we might get a hot shower in the morning as well.
KATE: Listen to him. For fifty-one weeks of the year it's as much as I can do to get him to take a shower once a week.
BRIAN: That is not true, and you know it, and I'd appreciate it if you didn't discuss my personal habits in front of people.
ROBERT: Look, if it'll make you happier Brian, you and Kate can shower first for the rest of the holiday.
BRIAN: What, and spoil the rota it took you three weeks to

devise. What happened to the 'organisation is the key to a successful holiday' attitude.
ROBERT: It's no problem, really. I don't mind. Honest.
CLARE: Talking of rotas. Whose turn is it to do breakfast today?
ROBERT: Look, let's just forget about the rota. It wasn't such a good idea after all. It's no problem with me, honest. Or Clare. Is it Clare?
CLARE: Well, it was fair. We did agree, so Kate and I wouldn't have to do all the work. It is our holiday too.
ROBERT: Clare, please.
CLARE: Oh, I don't mind. If it's all right with Kate, it's all right with me.
KATE: No. I don't mind. What about you Brian?
BRIAN: No. Stick to the rota. It took him long enough to work out, what with his slide rule and permutations. Whose turn it it anyway?
ROBERT: It's your's actually.
BRIAN: I should have known. It's not my day is it. Well, at least we have good old democracy to fall back on. Three-to-one in favour of scrapping the rota. Democracy wins by a short head. I'll have a bacon sandwich please Kate.
KATE: Oh no. You're not getting away with that one. It's your turn to do the breakfast. If you want a bacon sandwich, you can cook it yourself, and I'll have one as well.
CLARE: That sounds like a nice change.
ROBERT: I'll have an egg with mine, if that's all right?
KATE: An egg, smashing. I quite fancy an egg as well.
BRIAN: Hang on a minute. For the last four mornings, all I've had is a bit of French bread and jam. Now, all of a sudden, when it's my turn to do breakfast, everybody's got shares in Trust House Forte.
KATE: It was your idea.
BRIAN: That was when someone else was going to do it.
CLARE: You are so selfish Brian.
BRIAN: Me selfish. I didn't ask for bacon and egg when you were doing breakfast, did I? I would have loved a

bit of bacon, but did I ask? No. I just rammed another bit of boring baguette down my gob and kept my trap shut. That's not being selfish in my book.
ROBERT: All right, let's not have world war three over breakfast. I'll settle for bread and jam. So will Clare.
CLARE: But I want bacon.
ROBERT: Clare, please.
CLARE: Oh, OK.
ROBERT: Kate?
KATE: You shouldn't give in to him all the time. He always gets his own way.
ROBERT: Please Kate.
KATE: OK, OK, anything for a quiet life. Bread and jam it is.
ROBERT: Fine. Well, that's that sorted out.
BRIAN: We're out of bread. Whose turn is it to do the shopping?
ROBERT: Ehm.....
CLARE: Well?
ROBERT: It's Brian's actually.
BRIAN: Hang on. That can't be right. Give me that rota. Oh, brilliant. According to Einstein here, today, I'm supposed to do the breakfast, the shopping, the washing and wiping up and clean the apartment, while you lot do bugger all. What sort of rota do you call this?
CLARE: A fair one.
BRIAN: Fair. How can it be fair, when I've got to do everything in one day?
KATE: It's fair because you haven't done anything for the last four days. You never do.
ROBERT: The computer did take that into account actually.
BRIAN: Well, you can stuff your computer. It's not fair.
CLARE: Of course it is. I don't know how you have the nerve to say it isn't fair. We have done everything for the last four days. You have done nothing, except get blind drunk.
BRIAN: I did the shopping on the first day.
CLARE: You bought six cases of beer and nothing else.

PISTE OFF

BRIAN: Bare essentials you said and bare essentials you got.
KATE: Your bare essentials. The rest of us happen to exist on more than Stella Artois.
BRIAN: It's a holiday for Christ's sake. A man's entitled to have a few beers on holiday.
CLARE: Life is one long holiday for you Brian.
BRIAN: Look, what is this? National have a go at Brian day? Did you all sit up until two in the morning conspiring together, to pick on me today, or what?
ROBERT: No, it's just....
BRIAN: Just what?
CLARE: Well....
BRIAN: Well what, for Christ's sake.
KATE: What Robert and Clare are trying tactfully to say Brian, is that we, that is, Robert, Clare and I, are just a little bit unhappy about the way you have deliberately set out to ruin this holiday.
BRIAN: Me! Is it my fault there's no snow? What did I do? Stand out there spraying aerosol cans up at the sky to open up the ozone layer? No I did not. If anyone has the right to be fed up it's me. I've spent a hundred and fifty pounds on boots, two hundred on skis. I've got saloppettes, racing trousers and an all in one. None from C and A, I might add, and why did I buy it? So I could lug the stuff halfway across London just to stand around Gatwick Airport guarding it for six hours, while the French air traffic controllers decide whether they are on strike or not....
KATE: All right Brian, we get the message.
BRIAN: Then, when we finally touched down, a two hour journey to the resort, suddenly became six hours, because we're being driven by a mad Frenchman, who's as much use as a blind homing pigeon. When we finally arrive, I have to lug it three quarters of a mile up a one in ten hill to this rabbit hutch where there isn't enough room to swing a mouse.
ROBERT: A cat. It's a cat actually.
BRIAN: I was right the first time, thank you.

PISTE OFF

KATE: All right Brian, calm down. We get the message.
BRIAN: So, there it all sits. Like a Benedictine nun untouched by human hands, and not likely to be, for the forseable future.
ROBERT: I did tell you not to buy all that stuff. It's not necessary. Clare and I had been going skiing for about five years before we got our own. You might not like skiing.
BRIAN: Of course I'd like it. I was brilliant on the dry slope.
CLARE: You broke your wrist.
BRIAN: That wasn't my fault. It was that idiot in the pink outfit. He was completely out of control. He knocked me over. They shouldn't allow people like that on the slope, it's dangerous.
ROBERT: He was one of the instructors.
BRIAN: Then he should have been able to get out of my way. How do they expect people to learn the basics if the instructors can't even do it? Anyway, the man in the shop said I'd learn quicker with the right equipment.
CLARE: He would.
ROBERT: I said you should have let me come with you when you bought it.
BRIAN: I know what I'm doing. I'm not a complete idiot.
CLARE: Why did you buy two metre Rossignol slaloms and racing boots then?
BRIAN: So I could grow into them. It saves me buying new equipment again when I'm a bit better
KATE: Better. You haven't been on any snow yet.
BRIAN: I'm not likely to this holiday am I? We should have gone to Scotland.
CLARE: It's cold in Scotland.
BRIAN: It's supposed to be cold. It usually snows when it's cold.
ROBERT: Well, actually, scientifically, that's not true. It actually snows when it's warm, after it's been cold. It's something to do with....
BRIAN: Who rattled your cage?
ROBERT: I was only trying to explain....

PISTE OFF

BRIAN: Well don't.
KATE: Brian. You apologise for that.
BRIAN: For what?
KATE: Shouting at Robert, like that.
BRIAN: I wasn't shouting.
KATE: You're shouting now.
BRIAN: All right, all right. I'm sorry.
ROBERT: That's OK. My fault. I shouldn't have butted in. No harm done.
KATE: Now, for heavens sake. This is a holiday. We should be having fun. So let's have no more arguing, please. *(They all sit in silence)*
BRIAN: Anyway, you never know what you're going to catch using hire equipment.
KATE: Brian, I warned you....
CLARE: Oh, and what dreadful disease do you think you're going to catch from a pair of skis then Brian?
ROBERT: Clare, please don't start again.
CLARE: Well, it's him. He's being stupid.
KATE: No more arguments, please. Agreed?
CLARE: It's fine by me. Tell him.
ROBERT: Brian?
BRIAN: Fine.
KATE: Fine. Well, that's all settled then. Right then, who's for a nice cup of tea.
CLARE: Oh, yes please Kate.
ROBERT: Thanks Kate.
KATE: Brian?
BRIAN: I'll have coffee.
KATE: Fine. *(KATE goes to the kitchen area. The others sit in silence)*
BRIAN: I meant the boots actually. The French are notorious for foot rot.
CLARE: You do talk rubbish Brian.
ROBERT: Clare......
BRIAN: It's an historical fact. Well documented.
CLARE: Where?
ROBERT: Brian.....
BRIAN: I read it in the Sun, that time when they were stopping our lorries loaded with lamb.

PISTE OFF

CLARE: Oh, well, if it was in the Sun, it must be true.
ROBERT: Clare, please....
BRIAN: Sarcasm is the lowest form of wit.
ROBERT: Pack it in Brian.
CLARE: Did you get that out of the Sun as well, or have you memorised it from a game of quotations?
ROBERT: I give up.
BRIAN: No. It was in the Guardian actually.
ROBERT: I really do give up.
CLARE: You've never read the Guardian in your life. *(KATE enters with two mugs of tea)*
KATE: Let's not get into politics, please Clare. You promised.
CLARE: He started it. He always starts a political argument with the Guardian because he knows I read it.
BRIAN: No-one reads the Guardian. They just buy it and stick it in their bags so everyone can see it. It's like some secret masonic signal. Look at me, I'm a trendy intelligent lefty.
KATE: Brian, pack it in. Sex, politics and religion are taboo subjects this week. We all agreed.
ROBERT: I don't remember agreeing to that.
CLARE: You weren't there when it was agreed.
ROBERT: Oh, great. I don't count then.
KATE: Of course you count Robert. Clare said you wouldn't mind.
ROBERT: I do mind actually. Despite what you all might think, I am quite capable of forming an opinion without Clare's help.
BRIAN: The worm has turned.
CLARE: Don't you call Robert a worm.
BRIAN: Why not? It's about time he stood up for himself.
ROBERT: Yes, why not? Brian can call me a worm if he likes, or isn't he entitled to an opinion either.
CLARE: Oh, come on Robert. Don't sulk over a stupid little thing like this.
ROBERT: I'm not sulking.
CLARE: Yes you are. Your bottom lip's dropped. It always does that when he sulks. Bless his little heart. Give us a kiss.

ROBERT: No thank you.
CLARE: Robert, I want a kiss.
ROBERT: I'm not in the mood just now, thank you.
CLARE: Not another headache.
ROBERT: Let's drop the subject, if you wouldn't mind.
CLARE: It's you who won't give me a kiss. It's not as if I'm asking for three hours of unbridled passion or anything.
BRIAN: Three hours. No wonder you always look tired Robert.
ROBERT: Look. I'd appreciate it if my sex life was not open for discussion right now, thank you.
CLARE: What sex life. The last time a star appeared in my diary, it was my birthday. That was last June.
ROBERT: You're a nymphomaniac, that's your trouble.
CLARE: It's no trouble.
ROBERT: Three days without and she becomes violent.
CLARE: All right, don't get excited. I was only joking.
ROBERT: Am I laughing? Are Kate and Brian laughing?
BRIAN: I'm trying not to.
KATE: Brian.
CLARE: All right, all right. I'm sorry. I'm sorry OK. Kiss and make up.
ROBERT: There you go again.
CLARE: Oh for Pete's sake, I give up. I really do. What's the matter with you this morning? I'm going over the shop. Are you coming Kate?
BRIAN: Well, you're obviously not.
KATE: Brian will you shut up. Yes, hang on. I could do with a breath of fresh air. Perhaps when we get back, everyone will have had the chance to cool off and we can all start enjoying ourselves. *(CLARE and KATE exit. BRIAN and ROBERT sit in silence. ROBERT lights up a cigarette)*
BRIAN: Robert?
ROBERT: No.
BRIAN: You don't know what I'm going to ask yet.
ROBERT: Yes I do. What you always ask me, when we're alone.
BRIAN: Oh, go on.
ROBERT: No.

BRIAN: Just one.
ROBERT: No. You have given up.
BRIAN: Oh, come on. Holidays don't count. You're allowed to smoke on holidays.
ROBERT: Not when you've given up.
BRIAN: I'll give it up again as soon as we get home. It's no problem. I can give it up, just like that.
ROBERT: No.
BRIAN: Robert, has anyone ever told you, that you can be a real pain sometimes?
ROBERT: Me a pain. That's a laugh. You should listen to yourself sometimes.
BRIAN: I'm not a pain. When have I ever been a pain?
ROBERT: When you've got a couple of days free, remind me to list them for you.
BRIAN: No, come on. You called me a pain. When have I ever been a pain?
ROBERT: You're being a pain now.
BRIAN: That doesn't count.
ROBERT: All right, if you must know, you were a pain on New Year's Eve.
BRIAN: Rubbish. I was the life and soul of the party.
ROBERT: You were a pain, and you were boring.
BRIAN: Boring. Me, boring. All right I might be a bit of a pain now and then, but boring, no way. How was I boring?
ROBERT: Let's drop the subject shall we?
BRIAN: No, come on, how was I boring?
ROBERT: You really want to know?
BRIAN: Of course I want to know. I can live with being a pain, but boring, no way. So come on how was I boring?
ROBERT: On the last stroke of midnight, you crushed your last remaining Rothmans, over my living room carpet and declared to the world that you had given up smoking.
BRIAN: What's boring about that? Everyone does that on New Years Eve. It's traditional.
ROBERT: At twelve-forty-five, you were telling everybody how you were feeling much healthier now that you

were a non-smoker.
BRIAN: That's not boring in my book.
ROBERT: At one-thirty you started eating me out of house and home because your taste buds had suddenly come back to life. It was the first time in years you could actually taste the food, you said.
BRIAN: Did I?
ROBERT: Finally, at two-forty-five, you were actually lecturing my friends on the dangers of smoking to their health.
BRIAN: Was I that boring?
ROBERT: Yes, you were.
BRIAN: God, I need a drink. Is there any beer left?
ROBERT: That is why I am not going to give you a cigarette. I couldn't bare to go through all that again.
BRIAN: Why didn't you stop me? I must have made a right pratt of myself.
ROBERT: Stopping you when you're in full flow Brian, is as easy as trying to stop the flow of blood from a jugular vein with an Elastoplast.
BRIAN: Do you think you could sit a bit closer so I can smell the smoke?
ROBERT: Oh, have one. You might as well. You'll never give it up. You never do.
BRIAN: I will this time, as soon as we get home I'll stop for good. It'd be a shame to waste the chance of duty frees. It's the only time you get to have a cheap smoke.
ROBERT: That shouldn't worry you. The last time you bought a packet they came in fives and cost a shilling.
BRIAN: Get us a beer while you're up.
ROBERT: It's a bit early isn't it?
BRIAN: I'm thirsty. What else am I supposed to drink? Beer's the only thing I can afford out here. You need a mortgage to drink the coffee and the water's dearer than a bottle of Scotch.
ROBERT: You can drink it out of the tap.
BRIAN: Not likely. Have you seen what comes out of the tap? It's all brown and frothy.
ROBERT: Only first thing in the morning.

PISTE OFF

BRIAN: No, I'll stick to the beer, thank's all the same.
ROBERT: The wine's cheaper.
BRIAN: Wine's for wimps.
ROBERT: No it isn't. I drink wine.
BRIAN: I rest my case.
ROBERT: Why do you always have to put on this Macho image?
BRIAN: What macho image?
ROBERT: Beer drinking, womanising, foul-mouthed, describe most of your current attributes.
BRIAN: I'm not macho. It's all a front. I'm the quiet type really. Only no-one ever takes any notice of you when you're quiet.
ROBERT: You've never been quiet in your life.
BRIAN: No, deep down inside. The real me. This hard exterior is just to shield me from the outside world. I think it must have been something to do with being a middle child, or not being breast fed as a baby.
ROBERT: Pack it in. You'll have me in tears next.
BRIAN: I'm being serious. That's half the trouble. Nobody ever takes anything I say seriously. I've always felt different from other people. Not better, just different. I can't relax like you. You never let anything get to you. I've always admired you for that.
ROBERT: Thanks.
BRIAN: You don't care what people think of you. I wish I could be more like you. I wouldn't be seen dead wearing all that fluorescent make up you smother all over you face, when you're skiing.
ROBERT: There's nothing sexual in it. Everybody wears it. Men and women.
BRIAN: I'm not so sure. A couple of stripes here and there is all right, but pink lips - That starts ringing bells in my book.
ROBERT: It's only a bit of harmless fun.
BRIAN: I wonder if many transvestites start off on a skiing trip. A dab of make-up here, flowery outfits there....

PISTE OFF

ROBERT: Rubbish.
BRIAN: Don't get upset. I wasn't refering to you. There's no danger of you going the other way. Not married to Clare. No, you're all right. You keep sticking socks down the front of your racing trousers. No-one will ever doubt your sexuality.
ROBERT: There's no beer left.
BRIAN: Do you think the girls will remember to get some?
ROBERT: After last nights performance, I should think that is one item that's definately off the shopping list. Don't you?
BRIAN: Have you got any of your duty free's left?
ROBERT: Yes I have and no you can't.
BRIAN: Oh come on. You can't refuse me a drink. That's not fair. It's not everyday you find out you're a pain and boring.
ROBERT: And selfish. Give me one good reason why I should let you have some of mine.
BRIAN: Because we're friends.
ROBERT: Well friend, I don't remember being offered any of yours, before you drained the bottle on the plane.
BRIAN: You don't like Malibu.
ROBERT: Correction, I do not like Malibu, straight from the bottle. It would have been nice to have been offered one all the same. I could have mixed it with some of Clare's orange-juice.
BRIAN: Orange-juice. That's sacrilege. You wouldn't catch me drinking Malibu and orange-juice, it's a women's drink. I'd never be able to show my face at the rugby club again.
ROBERT: You're not a member.
BRIAN: It's the principal I was referring to, not the fact. Where are those women? I'm starving.
ROBERT: There's a croissant left if you want it.
BRIAN: Stupid bloody things they are. Only the French would come up with an idea like that.
ROBERT: Like what?
BRIAN: Eating cakes for breakfast. Can you imagine that in England? Serving Chelsea buns to lorry drivers in a transport cafe. There'd be a riot.

ROBERT: I don't see why. It's the same all over Europe these days. It's a lot healthier than a fry-up.
BRIAN: Tell that to a hairy-arsed lorry driver. He'd rip your head off.
ROBERT: You'd be surprised. Times are changing Brian. You're living in the past. We're all Europeans together now.
BRIAN: You may be a European. Me, I'm British.
ROBERT: Britain is in Europe.
BRIAN: This Britain isn't. I'm an independent nationalist, a dying breed. This is the last time you get me anywhere near Europe.
ROBERT: Are you going to sell the time-share in Spain then?
BRIAN: Spain doesn't count. It's not full of foreigners and it's got proper toilets.
ROBERT: You don't count the Spanish as foreigners then?
BRIAN: Of course they're foreigners, but you don't get any in Magaluf.
ROBERT: Of course you do.
BRIAN: Well, I've only met one all these years I've been going, and he was from Bethnal Green. *(BRIAN is laughing as CLARE enters with a shopping bag)*
CLARE: You seem to have cheered up Brian. What happened? Did Robert give you a cigarette?
BRIAN: No, he did not. I do not smoke. I gave it up at New Year.
CLARE: Oh sorry. I thought you gave it up every New Year. Traditional isn't it?
BRIAN: Where's Kate?
CLARE: She's talking to the ski rep.
ROBERT: Which one?
CLARE: The one with the nose.
ROBERT: Oh, that one.
BRIAN: You mean you actually caught sight of the lesser spotted Snow-Sure rep? Quick, ring up David Attenborough. I was beginning to think they were an endangered species.
CLARE: He's quite nice actually.
BRIAN: He has to be. It's his job.
ROBERT: The other one's not bad. What's his name? The other

one?
BRIAN: Ivor Nothercon, the rip off King of France, you mean?
CLARE: He's not that bad. I think it's nice of him to lay on all these little extras. He doesn't have to you know.
BRIAN: What extras?
ROBERT: He arranged a shopping trip in Monaco, on the last day. Then a trip to a perfumery on the way to the airport.
BRIAN: How much is that little lot going to cost?
CLARE: Fifty francs wasn't it Robert?
BRIAN: Five pounds to stop the coach en-route to the airport. Wow, what a bargain.
CLARE: It means going off the normal route. It's only fair that we should pay for the extra petrol.
BRIAN: It's two hundred yards off the normal route. God, he must be raking it in.
ROBERT: There is the perfumery.
BRIAN: You don't get it do you? These reps earn commission on everything you buy. It's just another way to rip us off. They'd starve if they had to survive on the wages they pay them out here. We're just a bunch of walking piggy-banks to them. The only time you see them, is when they're after your money. The rest of the time they're too busy working their way through half the female skiing population of Southern France.
CLARE: That's a myth. They're not like that.
BRIAN: Watch it Robert. The next thing you know, he'll be wearing your carpet slippers.
ROBERT: I don't wear slippers. Anyway, it's Kate who's missing, not Clare.
CLARE: Touche. So, have you two decided what we are going to do today?
ROBERT: Haven't thought about it really. What do you and Kate want to do?
CLARE: We could walk up to the Italian border.
BRIAN: What for?
CLARE: The rep said it's quite nice up there.

PISTE OFF

BRIAN: It might be nice when you're skiing, but what's the point of walking halfway up a mountain, just to look at another mountain? Sounds like a lot of hard work for nothing if you ask me.
CLARE: It's not like that. The border is on the same mountain. You can cross from one side to the other.
BRIAN: Oh, what fun.
ROBERT: Oh come on Brian. You could at least give it a try.
BRIAN: What for?
ROBERT: It's something to do.
BRIAN: Great. We trek three miles, uphill, in seventy-five degree heat, so we can cross backwards and forwards across an invisible border line. Anyway, how will we know where the border line is? We could be jumping up and down all morning. What's the point? You can't even get your passport stamped.
CLARE: At least it's better than sitting here all day, being bored.
BRIAN: What's wrong with getting a few beers in and playing Trivial Pursuit? We haven't played it since we've been here, and I packed it especially.
CLARE: I am not playing Trivial Pursuit.
BRIAN: I like Trivial Pursuit.
CLARE: Of course you do. It was made for someone like you.
BRIAN: Meaning?
CLARE: A trivial game, for trivial people, and if there is anyone more trivial than you, I've yet to meet him.
ROBERT: Actually, I quite like Trivial Pursuit.
CLARE: Don't encourage him Robert. You know he cheats.
BRIAN: I do not cheat. How dare you call me a cheat. If this was Las Vegas I could have shot you for that. You won't play because you can't compete with my superior intellect.
CLARE: You cheat.
BRIAN: You can't cheat at Trivial Pursuit.
CLARE: You can cheat at anything.
BRIAN: I do not cheat.
ROBERT: You cheat at cards.
BRIAN: Everyone cheats at cards, it's traditional.
ROBERT: I don't.

PISTE OFF

BRIAN: You are always the exception to the rule Robert.
CLARE: You're the only person on Earth who has taken the trouble to memorise the questions and answers just so you can win a stupid game.
BRIAN: Don't be ridiculous. How can anyone memorise six thousand questions and answers. It's impossible.
CLARE: If it means winning a game, you can.
BRIAN: Your trouble is, you can't stand being beaten by someone with only a G.C.S.E in pottery. It puts your degree to shame.
CLARE: Don't bring my education into this. *(KATE enters carrying a shopping bag)*
KATE: Now what's the problem?
CLARE: Brian wants to play Trivial Pursuit.
KATE: What's the point. You know all the answers. You've been learning them off by heart for the last three months.
BRIAN: I have not.
KATE: You have. I've heard you.
BRIAN: Rubbish.
CLARE: I knew it.
KATE: Most men sneak off to the loo with the latest copy of Penthouse. Mine sits there memorising trivia questions.
BRIAN: That is a lie.
ROBERT: I've never read Penthouse in the loo.
CLARE: You've never read Penthouse, full stop.
ROBERT: Let's change the subject, shall we?
BRIAN: That's right. We don't want sex rearing it's ugly head again.
KATE: Damn. I forgot the butter.
BRIAN: Never mind the butter. Did you get the beer?
CLARE: No, we did not. I don't see why your beer should come out of the kitty.
BRIAN: It's not my beer. It's our beer.
ROBERT: No-one else drinks beer.
BRIAN: That is not the point. The point is, we agreed to run a communal kitty. It was your idea Clare, if my memory serves me well.
CLARE: Yes, it was my idea because, at the time, it seemed

PISTE OFF

	like a sensible thing to do. I do not take into account your drink problem.
BRIAN:	What drink problem? I don't have a drink problem. I know when I've had enough.
CLARE:	So do we, you usually fall over.
KATE:	Clare's right Brian. It's not fair that they should have to pay for your beer.
ROBERT:	I don't mind.
CLARE:	Well I do. The kitty should be for communal items only.
BRIAN:	Well, if that's the way you want it. Fine. Let's have a look at what we have in here then, shall we? Oh, look. A bar of chocolate.
CLARE:	That's for all of us.
BRIAN:	Well, I don't want any more. So, that's eight francs divided by four, equals two, minus your three shares. That makes it, you owe me two francs.
CLARE:	Don't be ridiculous.
BRIAN:	No, no. Fair's fair.
KATE:	I'll have your share if you don't want it.
BRIAN:	No way. I want my two francs from the kitty.
CLARE:	Oh, let him have his bloody two francs.
ROBERT:	There's no need to lose your temper Clare. Brian does have a valid point.
CLARE:	Shut up Robert.
BRIAN:	Tea-bags. I don't drink tea, so that's another seven francs the kitty owes me. Washing-up liquid.
CLARE:	Don't tell me. You want your share of that because you don't do any of the washing up.
BRIAN:	I'll pass on that one for the moment. It's possible, you might be morally right on that one.
CLARE:	What do you know about morals?
BRIAN:	Oh look. Now, this is one item I am definitely not paying towards. I am not paying a quarter share in the price of a packet of sanitary towels.
CLARE:	They are mine. They did not come out of the kitty.
KATE:	They did actually.
CLARE:	Did they? Oh well, I was going to pay for them myself.
BRIAN:	Did I hear something about morals just now?

22

CLARE: Oh, buy your bloody beers out of the kitty. I don't care. *(CLARE picks up the loose change from the kitty jar and throws it at BRIAN)*
ROBERT: Clare!
BRIAN: Common sense prevails. I knew it would. So what is on the agenda for today then? No mountain walks, no Trivial Pursuit? Just another day of fun and frolics in flippin France.
KATE: I suppose we could make a start on the packing.
CLARE: That should keep us busy for about ten minutes. I haven't worn half of what I brought with me.
ROBERT: You never do. Every year it's the same. I think they should re-name suitcases justin cases. I mean, who wears dresses on a skiing holiday?
CLARE: I might one year. I brought them just in case I felt like dressing up. It's nice to dress up occasionally.
ROBERT: See what I mean. I brought them just in case. It's crazy, she'd freeze. Can you imagine it, all dressed up in a pretty frock and moon-boots.
BRIAN: I can see her now - Christian Dior dress and a pair of Doctor Martins. Quite attractive actually.
KATE: Why do they call them moon-boots? I've always wondered about that. I don't recall Neil Armstrong stepping out of Apollo Eleven in a pink pair of boots with a white fur trim.
ROBERT: Look at it all. Sixteen pairs of knickers. We're only here for a week. How many pairs of knickers can a person wear in a week?
CLARE: It depends on what I'm doing. Anything above a blue run, usually means two pairs a day at least. If I've been on a mogul field, probably three.
ROBERT: There's at least three different hats in here. Cans of Ralgex, nasel sprays and two pairs of goggles. Why have you got two pairs of goggles?
CLARE: One's last years.
ROBERT: What have you bought another pair for? What's wrong with this pair? We're not made of money.
CLARE: They clash with my new outfit.
ROBERT: What new outfit?

CLARE: The one you bought me.
ROBERT: I never bought you a new outfit.
CLARE: Well, not exactly bought me. You paid for it though.
ROBERT: It's great isn't it. Five years we've been going skiing and all I've got is one outfit. You have to have a new outfit every year.
CLARE: It's different for women. Men aren't so fashion conscious.
BRIAN: They can't afford to be. All their money gets spent on new outfits for their other halves.
KATE: Brian you keep out of this please. We've heard quite enough from you for today, thank you. If you two are going to have a row, would you mind having it outside?
ROBERT: Sorry Kate.
KATE: I don't know what's the matter with you all. The slightest little thing and you're all at each others throats. I'm surprised at you Robert. I've always considered you to be calm and collected in any situation.
CLARE: He is normally. It's only when he's had to spend some money he starts to fret.
ROBERT: I haven't spent any money, that's the point. You've spent it all for me.
CLARE: See what I mean. Calm down and stop exaggerating. You've been in charge of the money all week. I haven't gone over the days allocation once since we've been here.
ROBERT: I wouldn't mind betting I'll find a few Eurocheques have been used on my next bank statement.
KATE: For the last time, all of you shut up! I have had it up to here with the lot of you.
BRIAN: The lord has spoken. Right then Robert, are you coming over the shop to give me a hand? Or are you staying here with Madam Thunder?
ROBERT: I do need some cigarettes actually.
CLARE: Well, go and bloody get some.
ROBERT: Are you sure you'll be all right?
CLARE: Just go will you. *(BRIAN and ROBERT exit)*

KATE: Sorry Clare.
CLARE: It's not your fault. It's Brian. He has the uncanny knack of being able to wind me up without even opening his mouth.
KATE: You never have got on, have you?
CLARE: I try. Believe me I try. I just can't see how anyone can get on with him. He's so...Oh, what's the word?
KATE: Pig ignorant, bigot. Take your pick.
CLARE: You said that, not me.
KATE: Brian has his faults, but then, so do most men. We have our ups and downs the same as everybody else. But there are moments when Brian can be quite, well, exciting, you know.
CLARE: What, you mean....?
KATE: Yes, you know.
CLARE: Brian?
KATE: Yes.
CLARE: It's funny really. I've always thought of Brian as the whip it in, whip it out type. I'd never have thought Brian was the kind of man who would take the trouble of actually learning how to please a woman.
KATE: Looks can be deceiving. I have no complaints in that department.
CLARE: You should count yourself lucky then.
KATE: Yes, I did pick up the signals, earlier, that things are not going too well with you and Robert in that area.
CLARE: They never have. The problem, as I see it, is that Robert reached his prime at eighteen. I'm just coming into mine. It's like passing ships in the night these days. Mind you, he never was that good when he was in his prime. Robert's idea of foreplay, is a Chinese take-a-way and a bottle of Mateus Rose.
KATE: Men can be so romantic, can't they? It's funny really. Brian actually gets on with most people. It's just the odd one or two, here and there, that he just can't get on with.

PISTE OFF

CLARE: Like you and me?
KATE: Oh, we get on sometimes. The first three days of the honeymoon were OK.
CLARE: I've never understood why you ever married him.
KATE: He asked me.
CLARE: You didn't have to say yes.
KATE: I didn't have much option. My parents were away for the weekend and came back early. They caught us in bed together. Stark naked we were. Going at it like Jack-rabbits. I'll never forget my dad's face when Brian looked up, sweat, pouring down his face, and said "Hello Mr Green. I'm glad you're here. I wanted to ask for your daughter's hand in marriage".
CLARE: He didn't?
KATE: He did. Dad burst out laughing. Brian burst out laughing. Mum slapped Brian around the face and he started crying. My dad started crying and all hell broke loose. I just slid down under the covers, hoping the ground would open up and swallow me whole. *(KATE and CLARE are laughing, when BRIAN and ROBERT run in. During the following dialogue there is a mad dash to get clothed in full ski clothing)*
BRIAN: It's snowing. It's bloody well snowing. Quick, get ready.
CLARE: I don't believe it.
ROBERT: It's true.
KATE: You're joking.
BRIAN: He isn't. It's coming down really hard. The ski rep said we're going to get six inches this morning.
CLARE: That's the best offer I've had all week.
KATE: At last, thank you God.
BRIAN: Black runs here I come.
CLARE: Listen to him. Three months ago, he thought a black run was something to do with apartheid.
BRIAN: Clare, look. I'm sorry for having a go at you all the time, it's just....
CLARE: It's all right Brian. I understand.
BRIAN: Make up shall we?

PISTE OFF

CLARE: Right now I could forgive you anything.
BRIAN: Listen everybody. I just want to apologise for my behaviour so far this holiday. I promise you won't hear another moan or groan out of me for the rest of the week. I won't get drunk. I'll be nice to the French, the Italians, the whole world, and I'll use the toilet.
KATE: Amen to that.
CLARE: Come on then, what are we waiting then? Let's go piste bashing.
ROBERT: Hang on I'm not ready.
BRIAN: Last one to the lift's a wally. *(BRIAN runs out. KATE runs to the door and calls after him)*
KATE: Brian, be careful. You're boot's not done up properly. *(KATE exits. There is a loud crashing noise)*
CLARE: He's done that on purpose.
ROBERT: Oh no. He wouldn't. Not after all we've been through. *(BRIAN enters)*
BRIAN: Can someone get an ambulance. I think Kate's broken her ankle. *(ROBERT and CLARE exit. BRIAN slumps down on the sofa and starts removing his boots)* Trust a bloody woman to ruin my holiday.

THE END

LIGHTING/EFFECTS PLOT

LIGHTING TO OPEN: Blackout and stream of light shining through from kitchen area.
SOUND TO OPEN: Clock alarm bell ringing.
LIGHTING: Cue Kate - It's all right. I found it (Page 2)- Lights up.
SOUND: Cue Robert- Oh, yes, sorry (Page 2) - Alarm off.
SOUND: Cue Kate - Brian, be careful. Your boots not done up properly. (Page 27) - Sound of person falling down stairs.